T0114752

Academic Research and Writing
in Theology and Religious Studies

Published by

Mzuni Press

P/Bag 201, Luwinga,

Mzuzu 2, Malawi

ISBN 978-99960-45-02-8

Mzuni Press is represented outside Africa by:

African Books Collective Oxford (orders@africanbookscollective.com)

www.africanbookscollective.com

http://mzunipress.luviri.com

www.mzunipress.blogpost.com

Printed in Malawi by Baptist Publications, P.O. Box 444, Lilongwe

Academic Research and Writing in Theology and Religious Studies

Hany Longwe

MZUNI PRESS

Mzuni Texts no. 4

Mzuzu

2016

Foreword

For a number of times and at a number of postgraduate seminars and colloquia, Hany Longwe has lectured to our postgraduate research students in the Department of Theology and Religious Studies at Mzuzu University. The publication of this book offers a unique opportunity to share those insights into research processes and procedures with the academic world at large.

In this little book on postgraduate research Hany Longwe manages to put together, in a very concise manner, procedures and processes of doing postgraduate research in Theology and Religious Studies at Mzuzu University. While some of the specific rules and practices outlined here are subject to change or modification as the University develops new structures and procedures, the overall principles of doing postgraduate research will stand the test of time.

Although the text was prepared primarily with the postgraduate research programme in Theology and Religious Studies at Mzuzu University in mind, the relevance and usefulness of these principles will resonate beyond the discipline of Theology and Religious Studies to the broader field of the Humanities, and beyond the confines of Mzuzu University to the wider academic world.

I recommend this book not only to our postgraduate students in the Department of Theology and Religious Studies at Mzuzu University, but also to students doing postgraduate studies in the Humanities and other related disciplines elsewhere, and indeed to anyone who wants to embark on serious research in these fields of study.

Jonathan S. Nkhoma
Head, Department of Theology and Religious Studies
Mzuzu University
26th January, 2016

Preface

This guide is the result of recognizing the need for a general research guide for postgraduate students. It forms the basis for those working towards research-based MA and PhD degrees. I have witnessed firsthand, as student and as lecturer, the struggles and pitfalls students face in planning and carrying out theological research projects. That compelled me to put on paper that which I have learnt through the years in the hope of alleviating the frustration of postgraduate theological religious studies research students.

This is not a final authority in the field of theological research, but a contribution to a field that continues to grow rapidly. There are many good books on the subject. This guide is basically out of my experiences and others with whom I have taught and supervised academic research students in theology and religious studies.

The aim of this book is to empower students to do research and write better dissertations with confidence. The book has been produced to provide students with the basic information needed to understand the theological and religious research process, from the idea stage to the production and submission of a dissertation. It is expected that the work will satisfy the needs of theological and religious studies students who must plan a research project and carry it out to completion to qualify for a degree through research.

Although the work is directed towards Postgraduate Studies, its contents are also valuable for Bachelor students in Malawi and beyond.

I express my gratitude to all who have helped me. In particular, I am grateful to Prof Klaus Fiedler, my postgraduate supervisor for both MA and PhD. Many thanks for being an encourager throughout my studies and my daily walk as an academician.

I also thank my wife, Molly, a co-worker and companion in everything I do and wherever I go. You have been by my side when times were good and difficult and that has enabled me to be successful as a teacher and learner.

Many thanks go to many who I have taught and supervised in their research work. Congratulations for all the work that led you to where you are now!

Above all, I thank God for everything. Without him, I am nothing, but with him I am who I am.

Contents

Introduction

I obtained both MA and PhD by research. The research and writing have been some of the best experiences in my life. It is work, I agree, but it does not overshadow the benefits. It has allowed me to develop research skills as well as invaluable transferable skills which I apply not only to my academic life, but also to my work and a variety of vocations outside of the academic world. I have been able to interact with some of the best university lecturers and researchers from a number of disciplines, which has contributed to my transformation into a more confident and knowledgeable person. I have had my MA thesis and PhD dissertation published because my main supervisor and head of the postgraduate programme always told students that they needed to imagine that they were writing books not just dissertations. I published several articles, and one of them was translated for German speakers. In addition, I have contributed articles that have been published in handbooks on theological education and church history. As I prepare this guide, I have been requested by another university to contribute to that institution's companion's series that will comprise country-level essays. All I am saying is that what you gain during your study by research will serve you the rest of your life, because research is about curiosity or interest, discovery or unearthing and dialogue or exchange of ideas. I wish this type of learning was introduced early in our schools!

In our daily life we are involved in activities that have some of the characteristics of formal research, even though perhaps we do not realize that at the time. We observe, analyze, question, hypothesize and evaluate. But rarely do we do these things systematically or observe under controlled conditions. Rarely are our instruments as accurate and reliable as might be, and rarely do we use the variety of research techniques and methodologies at our disposal. The term "research" can be defined as any sort of careful, systematic, patient study and investigation in some field of knowledge, undertaken to discover or establish facts and principles.[1] It can also be described as "a systematic way of asking intelligent questions about important topics that yields dependable answers."[2]

From the above, a formal research is systematic, intelligent, important and dependable.

---

[1] Jack R. Fraenkel and Norman E. Wallen, *How to Design and Evaluate Research in Education*, Boston: McGraw-Hill, 2000, pp. 8, 9, as quoted in Douglas E. Welch, Merle D. Strege and John H. Aukerman, *Guide to Graduate Theological Research and Writing*, Anderson: AU, 2010, p. 9.

Systematic

Systematic means that the research is a carefully planned investigation, and the collected information is carefully scrutinized. A theoretical rationale which provides unity and cohesion guides the research activities.

Intelligent

The research is described as intelligent because the researchers question and re-examine traditions, other related research, and their own conceptual framework, and distinguish what is relevant from what is beside the point.

Important

It is important because the research contributes new knowledge to what is already known about a subject of study, in a way which brings positive changes in people's lives. As a result, research is worth the effort.

Dependable

In addition to yielding answers with approximate truth, research also identifies areas for further inquiry.[3]

Responsibilities

To make the best of your study, you must know the responsibilities of the different parties involved in your studies. Though these may vary from one institution to another, there are some general descriptions.

Responsibility for academic research and writing lies equally in the hands of the stakeholders, namely, the University, the Academic Postgraduate Committee, the Coordinator of Postgraduate Studies, the supervisors and the research students. Nonetheless, though the stakeholders are moving together, **the student is in the driving seat**. The other stakeholders will offer practical advice, but it is the students' responsibility to learn from their forerunners.

University or Institution

In relation to research students, the University is responsible to:

1. Ensure that students have the required entry qualifications so that they have every chance of succeeding in their research;
2. Guarantee that students have suitable supervisors for research studies;
3. Advise students of the facilities and resources which are available to them;
4. Inform students of the requirements of the research programme;

---

[3] Douglas E. Welch, Merle D. Strege and John H. Aukerman, *Guide to Graduate Theological Research and Writing*, p. 9.

5. Make sure that students know the grievances and appeal process;
6. Enlighten students about the details of the examination process.

Academic Postgraduate Committee

The Academic Postgraduate Committee is responsible to:

1. Administer postgraduate studies;
2. Approve the appointment of supervisors for postgraduate studies;
3. Approve the appointment of examiners for dissertations;
4. Appraise from time to time the criteria for assessment of dissertations; revise as appropriate;
5. Monitor the overall development of the postgraduate programme.

Coordinator of Postgraduate Studies

The Coordinator of Postgraduate Studies is responsible to:

1. Inform students and supervisors of administrative requirements of postgraduate studies;
2. Liaise between students and supervisors, and the Academic Postgraduate Committee;
3. Ensure that postgraduate students, supervisors, the Academic Postgraduate Committee, and the Registrar receive all necessary information and notifications;
4. Communicate with dissertation examiners and handle dissertation submissions and assessments.

Responsibilities of Supervisors

1. They will assist the student to develop a realistic and sustainable research programme which can result in a postgraduate dissertation.
2. To lead the student along the research process. To do research and to write a dissertation is not an examination, but a learning process, in which the supervisor has the leading role, but the student is the "driver."
3. The supervisor may recommend that the student undertake further studies in relevant areas as a bridging course or as a way of strengthening the student's grasp of the subject matter.
4. The supervisor has to develop the potential of the student and for this to develop the vision of the dissertation.
5. The supervisor is to exercise time control.
6. The supervisor may also use his/her initiative, and is obliged to intervene if the student lapses.

7. The supervisor expects a written monthly report or its equivalent in personal contact.
8. The supervisor will take care that the student writes proper English.
9. The supervisor makes sure that modules and dissertation are produced to publishable standards. The supervisor will make critical comments on the work.
10. The supervisor is responsible to ensure that the student produces a research proposal within the first twelve months of the study.
11. The supervisor will take care that the student writes with academic standard (in terms of content, language and referencing).
12. The supervisor makes sure that the student is aware and makes use of all the existing literature (even unpublished) and of ongoing research.
13. The supervisor will ensure that the student obtains ethical clearance when deemed necessary before the student starts to involve human subjects in the project.
14. The supervisor will enlist the help of other supervisors or assistance of members of other departments wherever that is relevant for a part of the dissertation.
15. The supervisor is responsible for regularly reviewing the student's dissertation and critically commenting on the work.
16. The supervisor will discuss any difficulties or concerns with the student in an attempt to help the student address these effectively. If for some reason difficulties or problems arise and cannot be addressed adequately by the supervisor and the student, the supervisor will seek the assistance of the Coordinator of Postgraduate Studies and/or the Head of Department.
17. The supervisor is to ensure that the student's final document complies with the programme's requirements for length and presentation.
18. Towards the end the supervisor must refer the dissertation to a second reader who will make observations, recommend changes or additions and assist in bringing the dissertation up to an examinable (and, wherever possible, publishable) state.
19. The supervisor will ensure that the student prepares and submits the dissertation for examination.

Responsibilities of Research Students

In addition to demonstrating the Christian character and conduct that the University expects of all students, candidates are required to:

1. Familiarize themselves with the University's regulations and requirements for their course of study and follow the guidelines in this handbook;

2. Work closely and keep in touch with their supervisor(s);

3. Take initiative in and responsibility for seeking solutions to problems they may have in your work;

4. Submit their written work and reports at appropriate times, and discuss and complete each section of work before moving on to the next section;

5. Take responsibility for the content, production and submission of their dissertation according to the specified requirements;

6. Participate in scheduled seminars or colloquia;

7. Meet all necessary ethical requirements in their research ensuring that they do not commence parts of their research which require ethical clearance until that has been granted;

8. Pay the fees for the programme, and for the production of the dissertation.

Procedures for Dealing with Grievances

A grievance is a behaviour or attitude perceived to be erroneous or unfair, including ridicule, inappropriate embarrassment, or work evaluation. Where there is a great deal of formal and informal communication, there is bound to be some damage.

General Treatment

1. Resolution and reconciliation is best achieved in Christian love with direct communication. The Department of Theology and Religious Studies (TRS) strongly admonishes students (and supervisors) to take their grievances before qualified Christians and not secular litigation (1 Cor. 6).

2. As the offended, take the initiative in reconciliation by going to the offending fellow and talk on a one-to-one basis (Matt. 18:15). The point is not to score points over them, but to win them over, and also to find out whether the problem you see is real or just a communication issue. It is vital to pray about the issue before trying to solve it bearing in mind that we must not sin when we get angry (Eph. 4:26; Rom. 12:18). You should lovingly correct them and restore the relationship before it suffers any further harm. Confront each other with true humility.

3. If you cannot resolve the problem, bring in a third person as witness (Matt. 18:16). To involve others in any disagreement increases the likelihood of the matter being resolved without damage to the relationship.

4. Only refer the matter to the Coordinator of Postgraduate Studies or the Head of Department as a last resort (Matt. 18:17).

5. Make every effort to preserve the unity of the Postgraduate Programme (Eph. 4:2-3). Never discuss your grievances with other people outside of

the conflict resolution circle. Gossip about the problems and talking to people on issues they do not need to know damages the unity of the body. Everyone is called to keep unity as much as possible. Matt. 18:19 stresses the power and effectiveness of Christian unity, not only in prayer, but also in other matters.[4]

Grievances of Academic Nature

A student may make a complaint or appeal orally or in writing. Oral complaints or appeals will be dealt with informally and complaints or appeals in writing will receive written response.

1. Complaints about the administration and assessment of a course should be directed to the Academic Dean.
2. Complaints about the administration of the university in general, should be directed to the Principal or Vice Chancellor.
3. Complaints or appeals relating to supervision should be directed to the Coordinator of Postgraduate Studies.
4. Any complaint on academic grounds shall, in the first place, be directed to the Dean as stated in no. 1 above, who shall consider the complaint in consultation with the aggrieved student's Head of Department. Such a complaint shall be made within 21 days of the announcement of the result.

The University will make every effort to deal with grievances through the channels indicated above. Provided the grievance was presented in writing, students who are not satisfied with the outcome of the grievance procedure, may appeal against the conclusion of the grievance procedure, in writing, to the Postgraduate Committee.

Develop Good Writing

To begin the actual journey of postgraduate work you need to develop writing skills. In order to develop good writing you need to plan, organize and then write. Through effort and practice you can improve your writing ability.

Plan

You will save time when you plan.

---

[4] The Sunday School Board, *Bible Book Study Commentary – Matthew (Part 2)*, Nashville: Convention Press, 1988, p. 29.

Understand the Question

Many students fail to answer or address the question because they do not read the question properly; as a result they lose marks. It is evident that students attempt questions in three ways.

- *Assume what the examiner had asked*

   If you do not read or properly understand the requirements, you do not address the key words used in the question properly. When you are asked to "examine", examine.

- *Assume what had been asked*

   Students may say, "I thought what was being asked there was ... and so that is what I wrote about."

- *Know the exact question*

   This is the only answer that will gain marks. In order to gain sufficient marks, your essay must have sufficient breadth and depth.

Find and Gather Relevant Information

Once you have understood what the assignment requires of you, you then look for information that will build up your answer to the question. How you use sources is very important. It is a common mistake among students to use the same source repeatedly as if it was the only one. Your supervisor will tell you how many sources are required for an essay, a paper or dissertation. The most important thing is that the sources must be scholarly, and you must be able to interact with the sources rather than just accepting what they say. Interaction means presenting your views as they relate to argument and topic under study.

Write

A written module or dissertation should have three parts: an introduction, a body and a conclusion.

The Introduction

The introduction states the intention of the writing, an explanation of what you are going to do and why it is worth doing. You want to set the tone of your work and that will be the criteria readers will use to decide whether to continue reading your paper or not. In other words, the introduction states the main or controlling idea that is to be discussed later in the essay. It clearly states the purpose of your work and argument precisely.

The Body

This is the main part of the essay. The body supports the main idea presented in the introduction. This is done in sections under headings and, if need be, with subheadings. The body develops the main idea in a logical and coherent manner. This is where your argument is given more flesh, clarity and precision. No unnecessary linguistic or technical ambiguities are required in this section of the essay. Diction, clarity and precision in language and writing are prerequisites to effective communication with your reading audience, particularly your dissertation supervisors and class lecturers.

The Conclusion

The conclusion states what was proposed and how the solution has been arrived at. It argues that the goals set in the introduction have been fully achieved. The conclusion is supposed to be short; your lecturer will say how short. Normally, for an essay it should be from a paragraph to no more than a page. Many students fail to conclude. You need to close the discussion without re-telling the story. Do not introduce new ideas. Do not use direct quotes, and do not introduce any detailed explanations. It is important that you tie your controlling idea to the findings.

The introduction and conclusion are very important. People are attracted to read the rest of the essay after they have been convinced by the introduction and the conclusion.

Inclusive Language

The use of inclusive language is much broader than the use of or non-use of "gender language." This may include the language of racism, ageism and classism as morally objectionable. Nonetheless, it is true to say that faculty and students alike appear to have more difficulty with gender specific language. Although many people desire to be sensitive and inclusive in their use of language, they find it difficult to rise above the old conventional linguistic practices. Regardless of the good intentions, the sexist language as part of modern English creeps on us without us being aware.

It is a fact that English is a wonderfully creative language; as a result, let not the force of conventional language blind you to that. If we learn to use language with creative intentionality, we can both overcome the linguistic conventions of exclusiveness and create new conventions which include all people.

It is commonly argued that lexical items such as *man, mankind* and *he* are **generic words**, which means that they are general terms that include people of both sexes. It has further been argued that the use of these words is not free from social and political influences, and they are socially constructed and sometimes socially manipulated.[5]

Some Guidelines to Inclusive Language

One way to eliminate non-inclusive language from our speaking and writing is drawing artistically upon the great range of creativity built into modern English. But we recognize that this requires sustained and determined effort by both individuals and communities. Here are some alternatives to the "generic" he:

1. *Recast the sentence in the plural, using* they, their, them.

For example: "A student will have an opportunity to select a book of his choice from the new acquisitions if he passes the exam with flying colours", becomes, "Students will be given an opportunity to select books of their choice from the new acquisitions if they pass the exam with flying colours.

Another way to recast the sentence in plural is to use *"they, their, them"* even when the resulting sentence seems to mix singular with plural.

"A person can help if he thinks his family will also benefit from the venture", becomes, "A person can help if they think that their families will also benefit from the venture."[6]

2. *Substitute the first person pronoun (I or we) or the second person (*you*) for "*he."

Instead of, "A student will have an opportunity to select a book of his choice from the new acquisitions if he passes the exam with flying colours", becomes, "You will be given an opportunity to select books of your choice from the new acquisitions if you pass the exam with flying colours."

3. *Avoid frequent use of the combined forms, "*he and (or) she" *or* she and (or) he."

4. *Use the gender-neutral "*one."

The use of "one" is quite appropriate in some contexts; however, over-use of it can make the statement dull. Instead of, "A student is considered successful if he passes the final examination with a minimum grade of 60 percent", it becomes, "As a student one is considered successful if one passes the final examination with a minimum grade of 60 percent."

Scholarly Writing

One of my very early lecturers in communication skills always said "good writing is rewriting." The more you write the better your skills in writing become. When you write, aim at communication, precision and clarity.

---

[5] D.E. Welch, M.D. Strege & J.H. Aukerman, *Guide to Theological Research and Writing*, p. 38.

[6] D.E. Welch, M.D. Strege & J.H. Aukerman, *Guide to Theological Research and Writing*, p. 39.

Structure in Writing

Good writing requires structure. Your writing must flow from beginning to end. The reader must be able to notice the starting point of the discussion through the relationship of the ideas to the conclusion of the study. Due to its nature, that is, technical and formal, academicians use some techniques such as triads, headings and footnotes.

Triads

At all levels of your writing, there should be three parts: introduction, body and conclusion. Triads mark the basic shape of a piece of writing beginning with a single paragraph to an entire essay, dissertation or book.

Paragraph

Paragraphs start well with a topic or thesis sentence. The topic sentence is usually, but not necessarily, the first sentence of the paragraph. This is a sentence whose main idea controls the rest of the paragraph. Topic sentences help the writer to keep focused and keep paragraphs manageable. They also help guide the readers through the arguments presented in the paragraph. Sometimes topic sentences can be used to connect paragraphs and chapters or ideas espoused in the essay or dissertation.

The body of the paragraph is made up of several sentences that explain, illustrate, develop or support the topic sentence's main idea. The paragraph ends with a concluding or summarizing sentence, which can also be used to bridge between paragraphs.

Section

Just like a paragraph, a section should have an introductory paragraph, a couple or several paragraphs making the body, and a concluding paragraph.

Chapter

A chapter should begin with an introduction, which is usually a paragraph or two. The introduction positions the chapter either in relation to the topic, if it is the first chapter, or to the previous chapter. It launches the theme or topic of the chapter and sets the tone for discussion. The body of the chapter should be composed of several sections that support or defend the main idea in a coherent and logical manner. The chapter should close with a paragraph or paragraphs that summarize the argument and form the bridge to the following chapter.

Dissertation

The introduction of the dissertation (or thesis) is the first chapter, which is composed of such aspects as the research problem, aim and objectives, hypothesis, and research structure. A number of chapters form the body, which presents a detailed discussion of the topic and an analysis of the data. The final chapter is the conclusion. Concluding chapters are not the only way to end a dissertation, and not all dissertations need a concluding chapter. Some dissertations end with a concluding paragraph or statement. It is a summary of the findings of the study and may make some recommendations for further research. It states what has been fulfilled and what gaps remain.

Headings and Subheadings

Headings enable readers to quickly preview the logic and flow of a piece of writing. Headings are used to divide and define each section of a paper. Some prefer four or five and others three level heading structures based on the level of subordination. Make sure you find out which level heading structure your supervisor prefers. Levels should indicate hierarchy of importance or scope of each heading and subordination. Two or more subheadings are required for each section—or else do not use any. Using too many levels of headings can confuse your readers. For short papers, two levels of headings should be enough and three levels for dissertations. Since the first chapter of the dissertation is a technical introductory chapter, it does not begin with a further heading.[7]

You can help your readers tell the level of the heading at a glance by numbering or stylizing them to distinguish heading levels. Always divide a section into two or more parts. A heading should not have one subheading, but two or more. Headings should complement each other. Equally, headings should not have only one subheading. If there is no complementing subheading, you might as well remove the subheading altogether.

In the process of writing it is advisable (by some Departments required) to use the decimal outline numbering system. For the published book it is usually better to omit decimal headings.

Photographs

A thesis must not necessarily have photos or other illustrations. But photos can be a valuable source of primary information and they can be useful in illustrating the text of the dissertation. For these reasons they are very welcome. The normal place for photos is in the main text of the dissertation. Each photo must have a

---

[7]   Klaus Fiedler, *Postgraduate Handbook*, Department of Theology and Religious Studies 2011/2012, Mzuzu University, 2012, p. 10.

meaningful and informative caption, for which a specific typestyle should be used.[8] Unless there is a specific reason, make the pictures small, and let the text run around it. If you have many photos, do not turn the thesis into a picture book. But since these photos may contain valuable information, put them as a Photo Gallery in an appendix.

Documentation

The strength of a thesis is in its understanding and analysis, of course, based on the facts presented, and these facts must be presented in the text. But sometimes you may have more valuable information than what you can put into the text. In order to preserve valuable information that does not fit into the text, put them into an appendix. Such valuable "surplus" information may be original letters, extended interviews of special meaning, autobiographical notes, picture galleries.[9]

Writing Style

Here are some general guidelines of style that apply to academic writing.

- *The language level must be academic.*

This means that it is *written in good* English, well understandable for the educated general reader. Avoid completely the use of "elevated" language. Scholars show their scholarship by expressing what they know in a way their readers can understand and appreciate, rather than expressing what they know well in ambiguity.

- *Write short and simple sentences in active voice.*

Wherever possible, do not write passive sentences. Maintain a thoughtful and confident tone. The research you are carrying out will make you somewhat of an authority on the topic. Others will cite your work; therefore, write with confidence and authority.

- *Avoid broad generalizations.*

Avoid using such words as *all, always*, etc., unless you really mean it and you have proof to support your argument. Otherwise, be specific by saying exactly what you

---

[8] MS Word proposes the style "Caption," but you may make your own choices. This typestyle must only be used for captions, as that will make it easy to generate the "Table of Illustrations."

[9] In my research on the history of the Achewa Providence Industrial Mission I found bits and pieces of an old diary. In order to preserve them for further research, I copied them and put them into an appendix to my MA thesis.

mean. Use the word "most" only when you really mean it, not when it should read "many."[10]

- *All good writing including research is about the need for truth.*

Truth comes on different levels, and you must differentiate these levels.

1   If you ask "Is morality among the Ngoni going down?" and the answer is **yes** or **no** or **partially**, these are mere opinions. They are true if you want to study opinions, but they give you *no information on reality*.

2   Perceptions deal with an observable fact, which is interpreted (perceived) in different ways. Such perceptions are valuable if you want to study perceptions, and on that level they are even a sort of truth, but do not mix perceptions with facts.

3   Facts are the things that *really happened*: that Kamuzu, of course not alone, dismantled the Federation, is a fact, but that he dismantled the "*stupid Federation*" is a perception.

4   Present your facts as they are; after that you analyze them. Only after that you may give your critical assessment.

5   If you describe something, like the teaching of a church, describe it first from the inside, then analyze to understand it, then relate it to other concepts, and finally you may give your critical assessment.

- *Use of the first person singular pronoun*

Don't write: "It is the present researcher's opinion." Instead write: "I believe." Write "I", not "the present researcher" etc.

- *Avoid clichés or colloquial or slang expressions.*

- *Contractions should not be used.*

Always write in full, e.g., should not, did not, is not. Avoid contractions e.g., shouldn't, didn't, isn't.

- *Avoid repetitions.*

Don't write "As I have pointed out before …" or "in other words."

- *Handle orthography with care.*

In Malawi we use English (UK) spelling and within that keep the **–ize** ending (evangel**ize**, priorit**ize** etc.). Americanisms like "**program**" *must* be avoided.

- *The necessary care has also to be applied to referencing (see separate topic).[11]*

---

[10]   Most means at least 50% of the total, but in most cases refers to higher percentages. Klaus Fiedler, *Postgraduate Handbook*, p. 8.

[11]   Klaus Fiedler, *Postgraduate Handbook*, p. 5.

Widows and Orphans

In printing the term "widow" refers to a single line or text printed at the bottom of a page, with the rest of the paragraph continuing on the next page. On the other hand, the term "orphan" denotes a single line of text at the top of a page, with the rest of the paragraph left on the previous page. Both widow and orphan lines are not allowed in your papers, both assignments and the dissertation. To avoid widows and orphans, activate the widow/orphan control in your computer programme.

Keep with next

A heading must never be left alone at the bottom of a page. Therefore activate the setting "Keep with next" in the heading typestyles.

Implementation of the Course and Learning Methods

Implementation of the course is through one-on-one interaction between the supervisor and student. You will learn by doing. Together with your supervisor you bring to this programme experiences that will add to the richness and relevance of the training. It will provide a forum for sharing information where everyone is a contributor.

Colloquia

The university will offer colloquia for research presentations and discussions throughout the period of your studies.

The colloquium is an opportunity for both students and supervisors to interact with others involved in research and to be exposed to, and consider and critique, research studies. It focuses on the student's work. This includes: assessing the student's progress; guiding the student on the next steps to take. This is done through individual student interaction with the supervisors and through the discussions and decisions of the supervisors' meetings; enhances the supervisor's work and experience, while supervisors' meetings enhance cohesion.

Every student is required to attend the colloquium and may present a paper or a progress report, be it a module, a research proposal, results of research. The student has to agree with the supervisor what to present. A text must be written and submitted to the supervisor, who in turn, after approval, forwards it to the Coordinator of Postgraduate Studies. Once checks have been made for the contents and level of work, the Coordinator will duplicate the paper for distribution before or at the colloquium. The student has to prepare a manuscript to speak from because there is no room for *reading* the paper. The presentation takes about 20 minutes, and should concentrate on major findings and arguments, not on technicalities like literature review.

Seminars and Mini Colloquia

In addition to the annual colloquium there may be other opportunities offered for students to meet among themselves and with the supervisors.

Currently there are mini colloquia every now and then for the North (in Mzuzu), for the Centre (in Lilongwe) and for the South (in Zomba). Mini colloquia are not compulsory, but all students should attend in their respective regions.

Recently two new seminars have been introduced: An introductory seminar for all beginners and a proposal seminar for those who have reached that stage, be it for a module or for a thesis.

Book Reports

In addition, the university requires that you read books and produce a number of prescribed book reports and write module papers in order to develop your comprehension and writing skills required in academic writing.

You will be required to read monographs, mainly those based on dissertations and write a 1-2 pages report on each book. In some institutions you submit the book reports to the Coordinator of Postgraduate Studies, while in other institutions you submit them to your supervisor. In any case, you may be required to copy the reports to the supervisor or the coordinator.

A book report has a heading: the author and title of the book; and the name of the student at the end. The contents of the paper are divided into three sections: about 60% of the report space is given to an overview of the content in the book, and 30% to deliberate specific points of interest, and the final 10% for an overall assessment of the book and its potential usefulness. There should be no headings or subheadings and numbering in the book report. The supervisor in certain cases may require the student to read additional books. **Always read one book, write the report and send it to the appropriate person**.

An Example of a Book Report

Masiye Tembo, *A Ngoni Story of Tragedy and Triumph*, Zomba: Kachere, 2005, 84 pp., ISBN: 99908-76-31-2.

This book is Masiye Tembo's narrative of the misfortunes and adventures of his maternal grandfather, Nemon Gumbo and his wife Jenara. Though not a thoroughgoing biography, the book has a substantial amount of biographical data for this Ngoni man whose Christian faith was a source of comfort and courage in the path of hardships, which he had to face in his short journey on this planet.

As a grandchild who was dearly loved by his grandfather, Masiye Tembo has again included some autobiographical data in this small book, as he tries to bring together the main pieces of the jigsaw that formed his grandfather's life.

While, agreeably, the book has no direct academic value, it is an interesting piece of literature for those that study the impact of Christianity on some traditional Malawian cultures it encountered, in this case the Ngoni culture. Again, in its description of the main character's journey from Malawi to Zimbabwe, the book portrays an interesting picture of the adventures of Malawian men of the pre-independence era in their struggle for economic survival in a world that was fast embracing a monetary economy at the peak of British colonial rule. The labour situation that became characteristic of the *matchona* syndrome points to a factor that revolutionized the cultures of Central Africa within a period of less than a century.

On a personal level the story is very moving and one that provokes the shedding of tears as Nemon's and Jenara's misfortunes are piled up one after another, especially in relation to the way they used to lose their children in circumstances that can only be described as mind boggling.

One of the most interesting things in the book is the connection between Nemon's family and that of the grandchildren of Mawelera Tembo, the first Ngoni convert to Christianity at Njuyu, well known for his compositions of several Tumbuka hymns still popular today. The author's autobiographical allusions connect the two families, as he is a grandson of Mawelera Tembo in relation to his paternal parentage. This book would therefore be valuable in tracing genealogies of some of the first Christian converts in Malawi, particularly those within the Livingstonia Mission's sphere of influence.

Rhodian G. Munyenyembe, Chancellor College, Zomba.

Modules

Apart from these readings and reports, you may be required to write a couple or more modules of 10,000 words or more. For an MA, 5000 or more is sufficient. Modules are sent to the student's supervisor. The student works with the supervisor in selecting the topic and area. Before writing the module, make an outline and present it to the supervisor for approval.

A module can be defined as a coherent, self-contained learning unit designed to achieve a set of particular learning outcomes. It is one of the requirements in the postgraduate research programme.

Written assignments form the backbone of learning and assessment in the universities or colleges of higher learning. As a student it is a must for you to learn how to write good assignments. You will not be able to succeed in all studies unless you put a lot of effort into good writing of assignments. In order to develop good writing you need to plan, organize and then write. Through effort and practice you can improve your writing ability.

Every module should present its sources properly and have correctly and accurately laid out bibliography and footnotes. Students should develop writing habits whereby they have impeccable grammar and spelling, a layout that is clear, writing that is free of jargon and to the point. Such skill often requires practice. The university takes that very seriously and seeks to support students as they progress in their communication skills.

Modules that are accepted by the supervisor will be made accessible electronically for further research, unless the supervisor or coordinator have good reasons not to do so.

The Writing of a Module

Here are some ideas about the writing of a module. A module is written in the same way we write a dissertation, but with less rigour and less scope.

1. Before writing, make an outline and present it to the supervisor for approval.
2. Produce Chapter 1 first. This is the "technical introductory chapter" and has to conform to specific standards. Whereas the main part of the dissertation should be written as a book, as if for publication, this does not apply to chapter 1. There is no exact prescription on how Chapter 1 must be composed. Much depends on the subject and on the character of the author.
3. Do not quickly proceed to the writing of Chapter 2 etc., but first make sure that you collect sufficient information from all available resources.
4. You then write your module except Chapter 1 as if you were writing an article to be published.
5. You include tables (only) if they contain information that is not already in the text.
6. Diagrams are welcome if they give information in their own right. They can be in the text or separate in an appendix. Each picture must have a meaningful caption.
7. Submit the text step by step to your supervisor.
8. Produce the final text carefully as approved by the supervisor.

Chapter 1: Introduction

The chapter begins without a further heading. In this text, in a paragraph or two, you take the reader from what they know to your topic.

The Research (Issue)

This section introduces briefly the problem(s) that you want to investigate. Use non-technical language, since the reader is still unfamiliar with the object of your study and with the methods you intend to use. The research problems are usually stated as questions. The normal length is one paragraph, two may be alright for special reasons or when *motivation* is included.

This section may well indicate your **Motivation** for undertaking the study. [Say "I", not "the present researcher."]

My Position as a Researcher

Indicate who you are *in relation to the intended research.* You may declare yourself as an outsider or as an insider, admit the problems and strong points inherent in your position. You may also include your Motivation here, if you have not declared it under *The Research Issue.* If you have done previous research on the same or a similar topic, you may refer to it here.

Present State of Research

This section is often called **Literature Review**, but since some research may be going on and has not been published, "Present State of Research" is more comprehensive. This section is not to be a boring (and neither arbitrary nor endless) list of books you have seen or used. It is to (1) introduce to the reader the literature that exists on the issue of research; (2) to give a brief introduction to the more general literature on the subject, and (3) clearly point to existing gap in research.

Do not forget to include unpublished material and ongoing research. Only include major literature (published and unpublished), to minor literature simply refer in the footnotes.

It is sometimes recommended that this section be written after the other parts of the chapter have been written and after you have done some work on the main body of the text.

Aim and Objectives

This part is compulsory. The **aim** can only be one sentence (though this one sentence may contain two elements). The **objectives** will all describe *intended actions* in the process of the research.

Devote one paragraph to the aim, then start the next paragraph with words like these: "In order to achieve this aim these are the objectives": Then number the objectives. Anything between 3 and 10 objectives may be expected.

Hypothesis

This is a fitting conclusion for Chapter 1. The hypothesis must be brief and precise. It necessarily reflects *expected outcomes*. There can be one hypothesis or two hypotheses, even more (but not many). The hypothesis must be formulated at the beginning and will be verified, falsified or partly verified/falsified, in the course of your work.

Methodology

This section looks different depending on the subject of your research. These are some thoughts:

- State somewhere early that you are using quantitative or qualitative methods (or a well-reasoned mixture of both).
- Be careful in the use of questionnaires. Make sure that they do not tie down your work to a shallow listing of opinions.
- If your research is more historical, a crucial method is periodization.
- Other disciplines use specific theoretical-critical methods, for example Biblical Studies research could use redaction criticism, narrative criticism, postcolonial theory etc.

In all cases you need to indicate the **sources**. Remember that these should not be a mere list, but indicate what the sources mean for *your* research.

Quick Guide to some of the Citation Styles

The purpose of citations is to allow the reader to verify and evaluate the sources you used in your paper. We cite or credit sources because we benefit from the work that has been done by others. Legally and ethically, you need to cite any information that is not your original output. To be a respected scholar, give acknowledgement where credit is due. In addition to acknowledging the sources, you must also document them completely and accurately. You must follow very closely the citation style for papers written in your general subject area, department or faculty. In spite of any documentation convention used, always check with your supervisor, department or faculty if modifications are made to the style. The essence of style is both precise and consistent. Whatever style you use, be consistent.

Chicago Style

The Chicago Style offers two basic systems of citation: (1) notes and bibliography, and (2) author-date. The choice of which system depends on the subject matter and the nature of the sources to be cited.

Many in humanities including those in literature, history and art prefer note and bibliography. The style presents the cited sources in notes and bibliography. The style accommodates a variety of sources including those that are less suitable for the author-date documentation system.

Those in the physical, natural and social sciences use the author-date system. The writer briefly cites the sources usually placed in parentheses in the text by the author's last name and date of publication. These short citations are augmented in a list of references where full bibliographic information is made available.

Turabian Style

The Turabian Style uses two documentation systems: notes-bibliography and author-date styles. It is a condensed version of the Chicago Style. The Turabian kind of citation is specially designed for students. It is often used in such departments as history and political science.

Modern Language Association (MLA)

The Modern Language system of citation is widely used in humanities, especially in writing on language and literature. It features brief parenthetical citation in the text keyed to an alphabetical list of works cited that appears at the end of the work.

You indicate the author and or title in the text of your essay and put a page reference in parentheses after the borrowed material. To avoid disrupting the writing, the MLA suggests you place citations where there is a pause, usually at the end of a sentence, but sometimes within a sentence before a punctuation mark such as a comma.

American Psychological Association (APA)

The American Psychological Association (APA) format is similar to that of MLA in two ways:

1. Parenthetical citations within the text and
2. A final listing of all references cited in the paper.

The APA style is sometimes called the "author-date" system because it requires that both the author and the date of publication must be mentioned in the text when referring to a source.

Harvard Style

It is important to recognize that Harvard is basically a business-oriented school. Some of the issues outlined in its Style Guide may depend on the course a student takes. For instance, if you are taking a business related course, then watch out that you use the appropriate guide or ask your professor, lecturer or supervisor which guide is recommended. In this way you will stay relevant by following the appropriate Harvard Style Guide. In fact, Harvard has several Style Guides depending on the schools they operate; so, it is most appropriate to consult the supervisor. However, the general rule that is common for the Harvard Style Guide is to use "author-date" guide for in-text citation. The Harvard citation style can vary in minor features such as punctuation, capitalization, abbreviations and the use of italics.

Kachere Style

In Malawi we also use the Kachere Style which is a modified form of Chicago style, and it is a footnote and bibliography system of documentation. This style is used by Kachere and Mzuni Series in their publications. The style only allows footnotes and no endnotes or bracket references.

Kachere Style uses footnotes for four basic reasons:

1. To give a reference to where you got the information. For this you must follow the Kachere reference style and do it carefully.
2. To give additional information that you want to make available to the reader, and which may also be useful for your dissertation, but which would burden the text unduly.
3. To advance scholarly debate, you may refer in a footnote to a divergent view or contradicting information and discuss it there and not in the text.
4. To refer to comparative material.

The following are examples of bibliographic entries and footnotes:

Oral Sources

Banda, Eunice, village headman's wife, Mtakataka, 15.4.2003.

Bauleni, Bamusi, pastor, Chifundo, Katete, 13.6.1997, 15.4.2004, 18.5.2006.

If used for a footnote, this is the entry: Int Bamusi Bauleni, pastor, Chifundo Church, Katete, 13.6.1997, 15.4.2004, 18.5.2006.

Correspondence

Phiri, Edward Chimutu, a letter to Charles Makwese, 9.9.1987.

Or: Phiri, Edward Chimutu – Charles Makwese, 9.9.1987.

If used for a footnote, this is the entry: Edward Chimutu Phiri – Charles Makwese, 9.9.1987.

Report Suzan Lungu, Blantyre, 2000.

Report Agnes Tito – Umodzi wa Amayi, 1997.

Report Samson Lambawanga – BACOMA Annual Assembly, Lilongwe, 29.8.1998.

If used for a footnote, this is the entry: Report Samson Lambawanga – BACOMA Annual Assembly, Lilongwe, 29.8.1998.

Correspondences with Author

Tembo, Rodney, London, email, 24.12.2001.

If used for a footnote, this is the entry: Email Rodney Tembo, London – Harry Joseph, 2006.

Chiukepo, Thomas, Johannesburg, 11.3.2003, a note to Harry Joseph.

If used for a footnote or endnote, this is the entry: a note to Harry Joseph from Thomas Chiukepo, Johannesburg, 11.3.2003.

Theses, Dissertations and Papers

Chirwa, K., "The Prayer of Hannah", International Theological Seminary of Malawi
    seminar paper, 2010.

If used for a footnote, this is the entry: K. Chirwa, "The Prayer of Hannah,"
International Theological Seminary of Malawi seminar paper, 2010.

Matumbo, Edward, "The Images of God and Feminist Theology", MTh, University of
    Lilongwe, 2002.

Chokani, Masautso, "Masculinity and Gender Based Violence", a paper presented
    at the Conference of Baptist Theologians in Southern Africa, Harare, 12-
    17.2007.

Pakwe, Penina, "Development of HIV & AIDS Village Support Groups in Malawi", a
    module paper, School of Theology, University of Nkhotakota, 2001.

Published Sources

Reference Books

Ferguson, Sinclair B., David F. Wright and J.J. Packer (eds.), *New Dictionary of Theo-*
    logy, Leicester: InterVarsity, 1991 reprint.

*[In most cases it is not necessary to put Dictionaries in the Reference section. If the
reference is important, it is better to refer to the named article.]*

NIV Study Bible 10th Anniversary Edition, Grand Rapids: Zondervan, 1995.

*[The Bible, the Quran, etc., will only be included as a Reference if that is an import-
ant piece of information.]*

References to biblical passages are often made in brackets within the text: (John
15:5) or (1 John 1:1) or (Gen 3:6) or (Lev 12:6-9). Biblical Books can be abbreviated
without dots. Make sure that abbreviations are used consistently.

Periodicals

Nyirenda, Petros, "Ngoni Chiefs", *Journal of Theology*, Vol. 2. No. 10, (July 2005),
    pp. 1-35.

Tembo, Martin P.H., "The Common Denominator of Criticism of False Gods", *Religion in Southern Africa* No. 12, (1990), pp. 213-231.

If used for a footnote, this is the entry: Martin P.H. Tembo, "The Common Denominator of Criticism of False Gods", *Religion in Southern Africa* No. 12, (1990), pp. 213-231 [11-23].[12]

Books

Amanze, James N., *African Traditional Religion in Malawi: the Case of the Bimbi Cult*, Blantyre: CLAIM-Kachere, 2002.

If used for a footnote, this is the entry: James N. Amanze, *African Traditional Religion in Malawi: the Case of the Bimbi Cult*, Blantyre: CLAIM-Kachere, 2002, pp. 127-129.

Baker, Robert A., *Baptist Advance: The Achievements of Baptist of North America for a Century and a Half*, Nashville: Broadman, 1964.

Bediako, Kwame, *Christianity in Africa: the Renewal of a Non-Western Religion*, Edinburgh: Edinburgh University Press; Maryknoll: Orbis, 1997.

Shepperson, George, and Thomas Price, *Independent African: John Chilembwe and the Nyasaland Rising of 1915*, Edinburgh: Edinburgh University Press, 1987 (1958); Blantyre: CLAIM-Kachere, [6]2000.

Web Sites

Slavery, htt://en.wilipedia.org/wiki/slavery, [17.1.2009].

Slavery in Greece, htt://www.crystalinks.com/greek/slavery.html, [27.3.2008].

History of Slavery, http//www.historyworld.net/worldhis/plaintexthistories.asp?Historic=ac41 [24.4.2008].

Preliminaries

We can now look at the process in more detail of how we get to write a module or a research proposal and then the actual dissertation.

Always take the ownership of the project by looking for an angle that makes the writing personal. The best research writing centres on your ideas that you develop through thoughtful engagement with sources. In poor research papers, the sources dominate, and the writer's perspective disappears.

Some universities require research proposals as part of the application or enquiry form. If you seek funding, you may be asked to produce something substantial. Your research will be only as a good as your proposal. An unplanned proposal leads

---

[12] Here the page numbers refer to the full length of the article, while the numbers in square brackets indicate the page(s) directly referred to or cited.

to a poor project, even if you are allowed to go ahead with the project. A good research proposal assures success for the project.

A research proposal is intended to convince others that you have a worthwhile research project and that you have the competence and the work-plan to complete it. Generally, a research proposal should contain all the key elements involved in the research process and include sufficient information for the readers to evaluate the proposed study.

Regardless of your research area and the methodology you choose, your research proposal must tell the readers what you plan to accomplish, why you want to do it, how you are going to do it and how the research is going to benefit the community or contribute to knowledge. The proposal should have sufficient information to convince your readers that you have a good grasp of the relevant literature and the major issues, and that your methodology is sound. Make sure that your writing is coherent, clear and compelling.

Choose the Area of Study

There is a difference between a dissertation and almost any other piece of work, and this is that you have to decide on the area of study and the title. For many students it is a daunting, troublesome and challenging exercise: Where does one begin from? Choose the area of study in which you would like to do the research.

The most important point about any research is that it has to concern something that you are interested in; something that you are passionate about. If you have little or no interest to start with, then it will be difficult to lift that interest should you encounter problems and a drop in motivation later on. You may ask: where does the academic motivation for a dissertation topic come from? Well, it may arise from personal experience: what you have gone through in your life; something that was supposed to be done, but was never done (that is what made me to write a history of the Baptist Convention of Malawi for my PhD); something you have read, or someone said, or you have studied or not studied; or your ministry or career aspirations.

Early in your project, get focused by narrowing your topic, brainstorming research questions and developing a working thesis.

Establish a Narrow and Manageable Topic

Good research is engaging and manageable. Narrow your focus to a specific feature or angle that allows in-depth research. Once you have chosen your area of study for your research, narrow your focus down to a specific topic that you would like to investigate. A topic is the main organizing principle guiding the work on your thesis. It offers you an opportunity for writing what you want to say. You may also ask: Is any topic acceptable? The answer is: Surely, yes! Nevertheless, it must be in the area of your major pathway; something you are able to handle, and suitable for the level of the study. Do not fool yourself, though, choosing a topic is not a quick or easy task. It may take time to formulate it. In many cases, the topic may change slightly or more as research develops.

Discuss the suitability of the topic with your supervisor. Also talk with people who are experienced in the broad area of your topic. Reflect on whether the topic is practical and useful. Begin with a straightforward, uncomplicated, easily read and understood topic. Be brief and avoid unnecessary usage of words. Eliminate unnecessary words such as, "The Case of", "An Approach to" or "A Study of." Use a single or a double title. Here is an example for a single title: "Women and Politics in Malawi"; and for a double title, "Life on the Street: A Young Woman's Battle for Survival."

The Delimitations

Delimitations are self-imposed limitations. They are the ways you choose to limit the scope of your research. You apply this to all sections of your study, beginning with the topic, the research problem and the scope of your research. The following are the kinds of delimitations that tend to form part of theological and religious study research.

a) *Canonical:* limiting your study to a selected corpus of scriptures.

b) *Geographical*: limiting your study to a particular region (or regions).

c) *Cultural*: limiting your study by cultural or language divisions.

d) *Historical*: limiting your study to a specific period.

e) *Ecclesiastical*: limiting your study to certain churches or denominations.

f) *Conceptual*: limiting the conceptual elements to be covered.

The title may include some of the major delimitations. For example, a title such as "Identifying causes of church splits in the Baptist Union of South Africa between 1980 and 2005" contains three delimitations – ecclesiastical, geographic, and historical.

Make a Literature Review

The first step in refining your research idea into a research question is to do a preliminary literature review. Make an early review to establish the context and rationale for your study and to confirm your choice of research focus/question. It is also important that you keep in touch with current, relevant research in your field, which may be published or not during the period of your research. The literature review will share with you the results of other studies that are closely related to your work. It also relates your study to the larger ongoing dialogue in the literature about the subject or topic, gaps and broadening prior studies. The gaps in the existing research may necessitate further study.[13] Carrying out a comprehensive literature review helps you to direct your energy and resources on real gaps and needs. It helps you to approach your research from an informed perspective.[14] The literature review presents a framework for establishing the importance of the research as well as a benchmark for comparing its results with other results.[15]

What Literature Reviews Should Be:

1. Exhaustive in its coverage of the main aspects of the study

As a Master's and Doctor's candidate you must show that you are familiar with all the major studies on each aspect.

2. Fair in its treatment of authors

Do not allow bias to creep into your research. When you are biased, your treatment of the sources in the literature review is often discriminatory. If you disagree with a source, you will not present a fair summary of its views and arguments. It may not necessarily be bias, but sloppiness; that is, you have not read the source, so you are unable to do justice to its contents. Consciously read the works you review and present an unbiased, accurate evaluation if you are to write a good literature review.

3. Topical and not dated

By 'topical' is meant up to date and of current interest. The bulk of the review should be devoted to the current state of research or debate.

4. Well organized and interpretive

A literature review should not read like an annotated bibliography, merely a list of works with a few words about each source, but should reveal your interaction and interpretation of it. You may organize the literature review chronologically, or by schools of thought, or by divisions of your study, etc. Whichever method you use must allow it to show your interpretive interaction with scholarship.[16] *And make sure that you refer to the literature wherever it is appropriate in your thesis, not only in the Literature Review.*

---

[13] John W. Creswell, *Research Design: Qualitative, Quantitative, and Mixed Methods Approaches*, Second Edition, Thousand Oaks: Sage, 2003, pp. 29-30.

[14] Kevin Gary Smith, *Academic Writing and Theological Research: A Guide for Students*, Johannesburg: South African Theological Seminary, 2008, p. 214.

[15] John W. Creswell, *Research Design*, pp. 29-30.

[16] Kevin Gary Smith, *Academic Writing and Theological Research*, p. 215.

Reading the Sources with an Open Mind and Critical Eye

You must keep an open mind as you begin to peruse through the sources. Do not let your personal opinions and beliefs prevent you from listening to new ideas and opposing viewpoints. Examine the author's assumptions, assessing its evidence and weighing its conclusions.[17]

Distinguishing between Primary and Secondary Sources

Determine whether what you are reading is a primary or a secondary source. Primary sources are original documents such as letters, diaries, attendance records, minutes, research notes and eyewitness accounts. Secondary sources are commentaries on or interpretations of primary sources. The advantage of primary sources over secondary sources is not their reliability but their being firsthand accounts. You can better evaluate what the secondary sources say if you have read the primary sources they discuss.

Being Alert for Signs of Bias

Just as you guard yourself against bias, be alert for signs of bias in the sources you read. Some sources are more objective than others. You will need to get expert help from, for example, academic book reviews and the librarian.

Some authors are more objective than others. If you have any reason to believe that a writer is particularly biased, assess their arguments with special care, testing them with your own critical intelligence.[18]

How to Obtain Sources for the Literature Review

You must understand that it is not easy to identify and access all the relevant literature. This means that first you must identify all the relevant literature for your topic, and secondly you must access most of the literature you have identified.[19]

Library Sources

Traditionally the library is the beginning point of research. Begin by acquainting yourself with the library and all its departments. The library has different collections. These include: references and indexes and electronic media. Although the library offers library orientation programmes, the library staff are there to assist you if you need help to find information and any other library related assistance.

---

[17] D. Hacker, *A Writer's Reference with Exercises*, Boston: Bedford/St. Martins, 2008, p. 380.

[18] D. Hacker, *A Writer's Reference with Exercises*, p. 383.

[19] Kevin Gary Smith, *Academic Writing and Theological Research*, p. 216.

Internet Sources

When you turn to the internet for information, consider what is credible. Use only authored sources since material posted on the internet can be questionable. The reliable domains are the *.edu*, *.org* and *.gov* sites because they are developed by educational institutions, professional organizations and governments. The *.com* sites are commercial, therefore, they are not credible enough to be cited in academic writing.[20] On many topics the first site to come up is Wikipedia. This has no named authors and the quality of entries varies. Wikipedia is not acceptable for academic argumentation, but much of its simple factual information can be used, for example in the background chapter of a thesis.

Formulate Research Questions

A problem might be defined as the issue that exists that leads to the need for the study. It may be viewed as a gap in knowledge that needs to be filled. The most important consideration is to define the problem as narrowly as possible; or else you will become frustrated because you have tackled a topic which proves to be quite unmanageable as you go along. Effective problem statements answer the question "Why does this research need to be conducted." If a researcher is unable to answer this question clearly and succinctly, then the statement of the problem will come off as ambiguous and diffuse.

You may formulate your topic in the form of a problem for which your research is meant to provide a solution. You must be able to formulate the problem in a single sentence. If you cannot, this means that you are not busy with one problem, but with two or more.

You must make the problem stand out so that the reader can easily recognize it. Sometimes, obscure and poorly formulated problems are masked in an extended discussion. In such cases, readers will have difficulty recognizing the problem and you will struggle answering it.

The research problem is oftentimes the first part to be scrutinized. Your whole work rests and falls on your research problem. You need to be able to clearly answer the question: "What is the problem?" Also answer: "Why is this problem worth the attention?"

Analyze your Problem According to Sub-Problems

Each major problem has a number of aspects which make up the problem. They are called sub-problems. These must now be spelt out one by one. A sub-problem is

---

[20] V.Y. Mgomezulu and F.A. Kalua, *A Guide to Academic Writing for Beginners*, Mzuzu: Mzuni, 2013, p. 14.

always a complete unit which can be researched, not just a question on research procedure.

Make sure that you only formulate sub-problems which are part and parcel of the main problem. Tackle one sub-problem at a time. All the sub-problems together must make up the main problem.

Never formulate more sub-problems than absolutely necessary.

Characteristics of a Good Research Problem

A good research problem must be:

- Feasible – *it can be investigated with available resources;*
- Clear – *most people would agree as to what the problem means;*
- Significant – *it is worth investigating because it will contribute to knowledge; and*
- Ethical – *it will not involve physical or psychological harm or damage to human beings, or to the natural or social environment of which they are a part.*[21]

Good research questions help you find information and ideas about your topic. These questions sharpen your research goal, and the answers will become the focus of your writing.[22]

Develop and State the Hypothesis

A hypothesis is an intelligent guess/forecast/prediction or statement of what the expected outcome of your research problem might be. The purpose of drawing up a hypothesis is to give direction to your thinking. Your research then has to prove or disprove your hypothesis. You must be warned that the formulation of a hypothesis tends to condition your mind in its direction, thus to presuppose the problem. So you must try to disprove your hypothesis as hard as you must try to prove it. Do not settle for a simple statement of fact about your topic; instead, choose a working hypothesis that seems debatable or requires some explanation. Note that your hypothesis may change as you research because sources may push

---

[21] Jack R. Fraenkel and Norman E. Wallen, *How to Design and Evaluate Research in Education*, Boston: McGraw-Hill, 2000, p. 30.

[22] Randall VanderMey, Verne Meyer, John Van Rys and Pat Sebranek, *The College Writer – A Guide to Thinking, Writing, and Research* Second Edition, Boston: Houghton Mifflin, 2007, p. 426.

you in new directions. In fact such change shows that you are engaging your sources and growing in your thinking.[23]

Once you have developed the problem statement and the hypothesis, every other aspect of the research will fall into place. You are on the way to produce a good dissertation.

Establish the Aim and Formulate the Objectives

After selecting your research topic, problem and hypothesis, the next step is to begin designing and planning your research project, the focus of which is usually expressed in terms of one aim and several objectives.

Establish the aim of your research. An aim is a broad statement of desired outcomes or the general intentions of the research. It underlines what is to be accomplished, reflecting the aspirations and expectations of the research topic.

Formulate the objectives once you have established the aim of the research. Objectives are a specific list of tasks or the steps you are going to take to answer your research problem. Usually objectives are numbered so that each objective reads as a unit statement to convey your intentions. Objectives are confined to what you intend to accomplish within your thesis.

Make sure that each objective contributes on how the aim is to be accomplished.

Method – How to Go about Solving the Problem

This section looks different depending on the subject of your research. There are basically three approaches: qualitative, quantitative and mixed methods. The researcher clearly and precisely explains what kind of approach she is likely to apply in carrying out a particular research. Subsequently, readers are kept abreast of what they should expect in the research report.

Qualitative Research Methods

Qualitative is an investigation that attempts to increase understanding of why things are the way they are in our world and why people act the way they do. It emphasizes collection of detailed information that brings meaning to the reader, and dependability, which is enhanced by the use of prolonged engagement with the participants (or with the archives, if it is a historical study, or with the text if it is Biblical Studies).

In the qualitative approach the researcher seeks to establish the meaning of a phenomenon from the views of participants. This means identifying a culture-sharing group and studying how it developed shared patterns of behaviour over

---

[23] Randall VanderMey, Verne Meyer, John Van Rys and Pat Sebranek, *The College Writer*, p. 427.

time. One of the key elements of collecting data is to observe participants' behaviour by participating in their activities. The study collects stories from individuals using the narrative approach. Individuals are interviewed at some length to determine how they have personally been involved.[24]

Another form of qualitative research, especially used in the writing of history, is archival research which may produce the main base of information for historical dissertations and monographs. Where possible, archival studies should be supplemented by information from other sources, for example interviews.

Researching and Writing Using a Qualitative Procedure

The research takes place in the natural setting, employs multiple methods of data collection, is emergent rather than prefigured, is based on the interpretations of the researcher, is viewed wholistically, is reflective, uses both inductive and deductive reasoning processes, and employs a strategy of inquiry.

- When using the qualitative approach, you have to mention the method of inquiry, such as the study of persons (narrative, phenomenology), the exploration of processes, activities and events (case study, ground theory), or examination of broad culture-sharing behaviour of individuals or groups (ethnography).
- The choice of strategy needs to be presented and defended.
- Further, the proposal needs to address the role or position of the researcher: past experiences, personal connections to the site, steps to gain entry, and sensitive ethical issues.
- Discussion of data collection should include the purposeful sampling approach and the forms of data to be collected, i.e., observations, interviews, documents, audiovisual materials. It is useful to also indicate the types of data recording protocols that will be used.
- Data analysis is an ongoing process during research. It involves analyzing participant information, and researchers typically employ the analysis steps found within a specific strategy of inquiry. More generic steps include organizing and preparing the data, an initial reading through the information, coding the data, developing from the codes a description and thematic analysis, and representing the findings in tables, graphs, and figures.
- It also involves interpreting the data in the light of personal lessons learned, comparing the findings with past literature and theory, raising questions, and/or advancing an agenda for reform. The proposal should also contain a section on the expected outcomes for the study.
- An additional important step in planning a proposal is to mention the strategies that will be used to validate the accuracy of the findings.[25]

---

[24] John W. Creswell, *Research Design*, p. 19.

[25] John W. Creswell, *Research Design*, pp. 205-206.

Suitability of Qualitative Methods for Theological Research and Social Research

Some of the reasons why qualitative research methods are appropriate for theological research include the following:

1. It has a wholistic focus, allowing flexibility and the attainment of a deeper, more valid understanding of the subject than could be achieved through a more rigid approach.
2. It allows the participants or subjects to raise issues and topics that the researcher might not have included in a structured research design, adding to the quality of the information collected.
3. One does not need to reproduce a theological research because the population under study cannot be duplicated.
4. Qualitative research methods are appropriate for understanding current social issues, which are of much interest for theological study.
5. Quite often, because theological research intends to pioneer new ground, a qualitative approach becomes appropriate.[26]
6. The qualitative approach is also highly suitable for historical studies.

Weaknesses of Qualitative Methods

Qualitative research method may have the following weaknesses:

1. It is possible that the researcher's presence will have effect on the people they are studying in that the relationship between the researcher and the participants may actually distort findings.
2. Some researchers can be overwhelmed by the information collected. They may become confused by their inability to limit the scope of their study such that they become poorly focused and ineffective.
3. An assessment of reliability of a qualitative approach is difficult because the research method relies on the insights and abilities of the researcher.

Quantitative Research Methods

As the name implies, quantitative research is based on the extent of quantity or amount. It is an investigation of things that can in some way be observed and measured objectively and can be repeated by other researchers. It employs

---

[26] Douglas E. Welch, Merle D. Strege and John H. Aukerman, *Guide to Graduate Theological Research and Writing*, p. 11.

strategies of inquiry such as experiments and surveys and collects data on prede-termined instruments that yield statistical data.[27]

In the quantitative approach the researcher tests theory by specifying narrow hypotheses and the collection of data to support or refute a hypothesis. An experimental design is used in which attitudes are assessed before and after an experimental treatment. The data are collected on an instrument that measures attitudes, and the information collected is analyzed using statistical procedures and hypothesis testing.[28]

Mixed Research Methods

Though research studies tend to be more quantitative and qualitative in nature, the mixed methods approach has come of age.

Criteria for Choosing an Approach

One may ask: What factors affect the choice of one approach over another for the design of a proposal? There are three factors one has to take into consideration, and these are the research problem, the researcher's personal experiences, and the audience(s) for whom the report will be written.

Match between the Research Problem and Approach

Different research problems call for specific approaches. A research problem is an issue or concern that needs to be addressed.

Personal Experiences

Students trained in technical, scientific writing, statistics and computer statistical programmes and also familiar with quantitative journals in the library would most likely choose a quantitative approach. Since quantitative studies are the traditional mode of research, carefully worked out procedures and rules exist for such research. This means that you may be more comfortable with the highly systematic procedures of quantitative research.

The qualitative approach incorporates much more of literary form of writing, computer text analysis programmes and experience in conducting open-ended interviews and observations. Qualitative approaches allow room to be innovative and to work more within researcher-designed frameworks. They allow more creative, literary-style writing, a form that individuals may like to use. For advocacy/participatory writers, there is undoubtedly a strong personal stimulus to

[27] John W. Creswell, *Research Design: Qualitative, Quantitative, and Mixed Methods Approaches*, Second Edition, Thousand Oaks: Sage, 2003.

[28] John W. Creswell, *Research Design*, p. 20.

pursue topics that are of personal interest – issues that relate to marginalized people and an interest in creating a better society for them and everyone.

If you are for mixed research methods, you need to be familiar with both quantitative and qualitative research. You also need an understanding of the rationales for combining both forms of data so that they can be articulated in a proposal. The mixed research approach also requires knowledge about the different mixed methods designs that help organize procedures for a style. For the mixed methods researcher, a project will take extra time because of the need to collect and analyze both quantitative and qualitative data. It fits a person who enjoys both the structure of quantitative research and the flexibility of qualitative inquiry.

Audience

As researchers you should be sensitive to audiences to whom you will report your research findings. These audiences may be graduate committees, conference attendees, journal editors or readers, or colleagues in the field. As students, you must consider the approaches typically supported and accepted by the institution. The experiences of these audiences with qualitative, quantitative and mixed methods studies will shape the decision made about the criteria for choosing an approach.[29]

Theoretical Framework

In quantitative research, the hypotheses and research questions are often based on theories, whereas in qualitative research, the use of theories varies. In quantitative research, an entire section of a research proposal may be devoted to explicating the theory for the study. In qualitative research, the inquirer may generate a theory during a study and place it at the end of a project. In other qualitative studies, the theory comes at the beginning and provides a lens that shapes what is looked at and the questions asked. In mixed methods research, researchers may test theories and generate them. Moreover, mixed methods research may contain a theoretical framework that guides the entire research.[30]

In quantitative research, you can use theory deductively and place it toward the beginning of the plan for a study. With the objective of testing or verifying a theory rather than developing it, the researcher advances a theory, collects data to test it, and reflects on the confirmation or disconfirmation of the theory by the results. The theory becomes a framework for the entire study, an organizing model for the

---

John W. Creswell, *Research Design*, pp. 21-22.

[30] John W. Creswell, *Research Design*, p. 119.

research questions or hypotheses and for the data collection procedure. A general guide is to introduce the theory early in the plan of study.[31]

Qualitative researchers use theory in their studies in several ways. They employ theory as a broad explanation much like in quantitative research. The theory provides an explanation for the behaviour and attitudes, and it may be complete with variables, constructs and hypotheses. Alternatively, qualitative researchers increasingly use a theoretical framework to guide their study and raise the questions they would like to address.[32]

Some qualitative studies do not employ any explicit theory as is often the case in history. Advice on theory use in a qualitative proposal is this:

1. Decide if theory is to be used in the qualitative proposal.
2. If it is used, then identify how the theory will be used in the study, such as an up-front explanation, as an end point, or as an advocacy lens.
3. Locate the theory in the proposal in a manner consistent with its use.[33]

Mixed methods studies may include theory deductively in theory testing and verification or inductively as in an emerging theory pattern. In either situation, the use of theory may be directed by the emphasis on either quantitative or qualitative approaches in the mixed methods research. Another way to think about theory in mixed methods research is the use of a theoretical framework to guide the study.[34]

Ethical Clearance

Chambers Twentieth Century Dictionary defines ethical as "professional standards of conduct." What researchers consider as ethical is very much a matter of agreement among them.[35] Ethical principles require that as you develop your information collection techniques or investigation, you need to consider whether your research procedures are likely to cause any physical or emotional harm, which may be caused by:

1. Allowing personal information to be made public that the informant would want to be kept confidential;

2. Failing to observe or respect certain cultural values, traditions or taboos that the informant values;

---

[31] John W. Creswell, *Research Design*, p. 126.

[32] John W. Creswell, *Research Design*, p. 131.

[33] John W. Creswell, *Research Design*, p. 134.

[34] John W. Creswell, *Research Design*, p. 136.

[35] Jack Fraenkel and Norman Wallen, *How to Design and Evaluate Research in Education*, p. 41.

3. Violating the informant's right to privacy by posing sensitive questions or by unlawfully gaining access to records which contain personal information;

4. Observing the private behaviour of human sources without them being aware.

Methods for Dealing with Ethical Issues

1. Obtain informed (conversant) consent of individuals who may be exposed to any risk before the study or the interview begins;

2. Do not explore sensitive issues before a good relationship has been established with the informant;

3. Ensure the confidentiality of the information, where this is required;

4. Learn enough about the culture of the informants to ensure it is respected during the information collection process.

Ethical Acceptability

Review the research you are proposing and consider these important ethical issues:

1. How acceptable is the research to those who will be studied?

2. Can informed consent be obtained from the research subjects?

3. Will the results be shared with those who are being studied?

Ethics and Qualitative Research

Qualitative research involves information that is recorded in narrative descriptions, not numbers. For example, the theological researcher uses qualitative method to observe and describe conditions rather than control them.

A Basic Ethical Principle for Qualitative Research

An important strength of observation research is the study of participants' routine behaviours within their natural surroundings. Therefore, as a researcher do not interfere with the natural setting under study.

Participant and Non-Participant Observation

Participant and non-participant observations are integral components of qualitative research and are used widely in theological research and also in the fields of anthropology, education and sociology.

In participant and non-participant observations you need to get informed consent if required because there is a substantial threat to privacy.

Unique Ethical Challenges from Participant Observation

Safety and protection of human rights are mainly achieved by using the process of informed consent.

Consent

As a participant observer you may directly probe into many facets of the lifestyle of the participants: their public and private lives and this is often sensitive. With such an all-encompassing capacity of observation, inevitably you invade on your participants' privacy. It is absolutely necessary in this situation for you to get informed consent. Some difficulties with regard to consent include:

1. The participant research methodology often requires that only the core group of participants know that the researcher is not just another member of the group. Is it adequate for you to obtain consent only from the group leader, for example, the head of the denomination, the chief or the pastor?

2. Another problem is the effects of obtaining consent on the behaviour of those being studied. By obtaining consent, you may alter the participants' routine behaviours. You have to keep an eye on the changes in the regular behaviour and the interactions of the group.

Those under observation may become increasingly comfortable with the researcher's presence such that they may forget that they are being studied.

Privacy

When you collect and analyze sensitive information it means in effect you are invading privacy. This is a considerable risk in qualitative research. One way you can circumvent privacy problems is by keeping the identity of your participants anonymous. Whenever possible, the names of the participants should be removed from all information collection forms, and other forms of identification, such as letters and numbers or alphabetical letters assigned, instead. Assure all the participants that any information collected about them will be held in confidence. Participants have the right to withdraw from the study or to request that the information collected about them not be made use of or made public.

Fieldwork

Information collection is a very important aspect of the study and it requires that you are accurate and careful in the process. Make notes from all your sources. Keep to your research problem. Any good material that is not directly related to your topic should be put in the "parking lot." You or another researcher may use it for a different topic. If you are doing qualitative research, you must plan to be on the field for enough time to collect good information. Carefully and critically present your information. What people believe is not what they necessarily practice, that is, keep in mind that things are not always what they seem.

An Overview of Information Collection

You must be systematic in your information collection. If you collect information randomly, it will be difficult for you to answer your research question convincingly. Information collection techniques allow the researcher to systematically collect information about the subject of study. There are various empirical information collection techniques that can be used. These include:

1. Print and Electronic Libraries
2. Archives
3. Interviews
4. Focus Groups
5. Observation
6. Participant Observation
7. Using available information
8. Written (Self-Administered) Questionnaires
9. Case Study
10. Life histories
11. Survey

Print and Electronic Libraries

Although this is a computer age, print libraries remain the most obvious source of information. Begin by collecting information from books and journals in your libraries. Try to find recent scholarly works because they are well researched. Journal articles that have been reviewed are sometimes better than books because they deal with more current issues; books take time to produce. Make it a habit to ask professional library staff to assist you in your research because they will save you hours of work. You can also go online for more books, journals and articles. If you do, make sure that the sources are credible. There are many substandard works on the web. You must critique what you read. Do not just accept everything you read. Ask yourself whether you agree or disagree with the author, and why. By so doing you are furthering your understanding and you open up new lines of inquiry.

Interviews

You will find out that interviews are undoubtedly a common source of information in qualitative research. An interview information collection technique involves oral questioning of respondents, either individually or as a group. You can record by writing down answers to the questions posed during an interview. You may do that during or immediately after the interview, or by tape-recording the responses, or by a combination of both. Interviews can be conducted with a varying degree of flexibility.

Interviews range from the highly structured style, in which you use questions predetermined before the interview, to the open-ended, conversational format.

For the most part, interviews are more open-ended and less structured. Normally you will ask the same questions for all the participants. Because the interviews are open-ended and less structured, the order of the questions, the exact wording may vary considerably. It is common that you may have to come back and ask more questions after the first round to clarify certain issues from a specific respondent or group.

During my history research, whenever I felt that I was not satisfied with the answers, or that the answers created more questions, I went back and asked the respondent or group to clarify. Sometimes it was just that they were not forth-coming in their response; but if deep down I felt they were holding back information, I went back.

You must first establish rapport with the respondents. If the participants do not trust you, they will not open up and tell you what you want to know. Remember that complete rapport is established over time as people get to know and trust one another.

You need to quickly learn how to ask questions in such a way that the respondents believe that they can talk freely. Sharing something about yourself or on related topics you know, may help to establish rapport and trust.

The person-to-person or face-to-face format is most prevalent, but occasionally group interviews and focus groups are conducted. A focus group discussion allows a group to freely discuss certain subjects with your guidance.

Focus Groups

You may make use of interviews on a specific topic with a small group of people, called a focus group that is usually homogeneous, such as church members, women's guild, or youth group. Using this technique allows you to gather information about several people in a session.

I have discovered that focus group interviews at time provide quality controls because participants tend to provide checks and balances on one another that can serve to curb false or extreme views. At the same time, because of the group setting, focus group interviews are enjoyable for the participants, and they may be less fearful of being evaluated by you the researcher. The group members get to hear what others have to say that may stimulate the individuals to rethink their own views. Because it is an interview, you are not trying to persuade the focus group to reach a consensus.

To overcome the problem of taking notes during a focus group interview, you may use an audio or video recorder.

Observation

Observation as a qualitative information collection technique generally is time consuming. You will spend a prolonged time in the setting. You will have to systematically select, watch and record behaviour and characteristics of people and situations or phenomena. You can observe in two different ways:

1. Participant observation in which you as a researcher take part in the situation you are observing, or

2. Non-participant observation in which you watch the situation, openly or concealed, but do not participate.

One major drawback to this observation technique is obtrusiveness or intrusion. You are seen as a stranger or you may feel that you are a stranger with a pad and a pen or a camera trying to record what you are seeing or hearing or experiencing. Your task as a researcher is to make sure that the participants become accustomed to having you around. You may want to visit the people and the site to gradually or quickly reduce this notion of "stranger" a couple of times before the initial information meeting. Your presence in the setting can make your participants change some things, and to slow down. You need to be in the setting long enough so that you are no longer regarded as an intruder. You can get the most accurate information if you can become "one among many."

Available information

Among the many sources of information in qualitative research is a large amount of information that has already been collected by others. You will need to locate and retrieve the information as a good starting point in your information collection effort. You may use printed materials such as course materials, rosters, reports, photographs and newspapers as research information.

It is not always easy to get access to existing information, but if it is possible, get it or go to wherever it is found and get it. The advantage of existing information is that collection is usually inexpensive, but it can also be expensive. Sometimes the available information will require a lot of time to collect, because you may need to organize it yourself in order for you to make sense of it.

The use of key informants, such as knowledgeable church leaders, members, youth, male and female, is another important technique to gain access to available information. You can involve them at various stages of your research.

Written Questionnaires

A written questionnaire, also referred to as a self-administered questionnaire, is an information collecting tool in which questions are presented that are to be answered by the respondents in written form. You can administer it in different ways such as by:

1. Mailing questionnaires with clear instructions on how to answer the questions and asking for mailed responses;

2. Gathering all or part of the respondents in one place at one time, giving oral or written instructions, and letting the respondents fill out the questionnaires; or

3. Hand-delivering questionnaires to respondents and collecting them later.

You must keep in mind that the results from written questionnaires often present opinions rather than facts.

Case Study

A case study is the collection and presentation of detailed information about a particular participant or small group from which conclusions are drawn only about that participant and only in that context. The researcher places emphasis on exploration and description.

Survey

A survey is a non-experimental, descriptive research tool for collecting information that is used to provide a general overview of a representative sample of a large population. The information is usually collected through the use of questionnaires, although sometimes through direct interviews of subjects. The researcher can use qualitative or quantitative procedures. Some surveys can profit from the use of population records, like parish or court records.

Importance of Combining Different Information Collection Techniques

The different information collecting techniques can complement each other. If you use them skillfully, they will reduce the chance of bias and you will get a more comprehensive understanding of the issue under study.

Bias in Information Collection

Bias in information collection is a distortion in the collected information so that it does not represent reality. Possible sources of bias during information collection include:

Observer Bias

Observer bias can easily occur when conducting observations or utilizing loosely structured interviews. The risk is that you may only see or hear things that you are interested in and miss information that is critical to your research. If you use research assistants to collect the information, one way will be to send them out in pairs when using flexible research techniques and make them discuss and interpret the information immediately after collecting it. Another way would be to use a tape recorder and transcribe verbatim.

Effect of the Interview upon the Informant

This is possible in all interview situations. The informant may mistrust the intention of the interview and dodge certain questions or give misleading answers. Such bias can be reduced by adequately introducing the purpose of the study to the informants by phrasing questions on sensitive issues in a positive way or by taking sufficient time for the interview and by assuring the informants that the information collected will be confidential.

Information Bias

There are cases in which the information itself has weaknesses. The information may have gaps or be unreadable.

Another information bias is due to gaps in people's memory; this is called *memory* or *recall* bias.

Defective Questionnaires

Defective questionnaires are those with:

- Open-ended questions without guidelines on how to ask or answer the questions
- Vaguely phrased questions
- 'Lead questions' that cause the respondent to believe one answer would be preferred over another
- Questions placed in an illogical order.

Defective questionnaires can be prevented by carefully planning the information collection process and by pre-testing the questionnaire.

A Word of Caution on Biases

All these biases will threaten the validity of your research. By being aware of them, it is possible to a certain degree to prevent them. If you do not fully succeed, it is important to report honestly in what ways the information may be biased, and what limitations there may be.

Writing up the Research

You will soon discover that writing up your thesis takes a considerable amount of time. Do not underestimate how long it will take to write your research. Once you have collected the relevant information allow yourself ample time to write, reflect and rewrite. Do not fool yourself that you will write up a good paper in one go. Every work can be improved. It is said that, "Good writing is re-writing", and hold that throughout your research career.

Your dissertation should include:

A Preliminary Section

This includes:

1. A title page (see Figure 2) on which is written the title of the dissertation, the name of the institution, the name of the degree for which your work is being submitted, your name and the date of submission. Following a coursework component, it will read, "in partial fulfillment of the requirements for the degree of ..." For a research only course, it will also read, "in partial fulfillment of the requirements for the degree of ..."

2. A declaration that the work is original and has not been submitted for a qualification elsewhere; some universities also require a declaration by the supervisor (on the same page) that it is submitted with her or his approval.

3. An abstract: a summary of the dissertation; summarizes the problem, participants, hypotheses, methods used, outcomes and conclusions. You state what you did, why you did it, what you found out and why the findings are significant. The length should be between 250 and 400 words.

4. Dedication (not compulsory)

5. Acknowledgments of any help you have received or work included that was carried out by another researcher or organization

6. A table of contents (This *must* be generated by MS Word from the heading typestyles used)

Where appropriate, the following are included in the table of contents:

7. Abbreviations;

8. Definitions
   Researchers define terms so that readers can understand the term's precise meaning. Whether a term should be defined is a matter of judgment. In dissertations and thesis proposals, terms typically are defined in a special section of the study. You must be precise in how you use language and terms. Here are some suggestions on how you may define terms:

   a) Define a term when it first appears in the text.
   b) Write definitions at a specific operational or applied level.
   c) Do not define the terms in everyday language; instead, use accepted language available in the research literature.

Researchers might define terms with different intents, aims or purposes. Although there is no one format for defining terms, one approach is to develop a separate section called: Definitions or Definition of Terms. Typically, this separate section should not be too long.[36] You can see how I have done it in my book *Christians by Grace – Baptists by Choice*, pp. 7-19.

9. List of illustrations;

10. List of tables

The Main Section

This is the main body of the text which varies considerably in format depending upon your study. Each chapter starts with a new page. But find below a few general rules that may help you in structuring *your* dissertation.

An Introduction

The first chapter with the heading: "Chapter One: Introduction" has a prescribed format. Depending on the system followed, Chapter 1 may deal with all "technical" issues like aim and objectives, literature, methods and hypothesis.

The Main Body of the Text

The number of chapters may vary greatly. But all chapters (except Introduction and Conclusion) must be approximately equal in length. If a chapter seems to be too long or too short, consider that to be an encouragement to restructure your dissertation. Chapter headings (except for chapter 1) must be substantive, not technical. Often the use of sub-headings is useful. Do not put a heading and a subheading immediately following each other without anything written between them. There must be some introductory remarks before a subheading. One paragraph is not enough to support the subheading; otherwise there is no need for a subheading.

The Concluding Section

If you include a final chapter "Conclusion", make sure that it is not a repetition of your work, but that it leads away from the text. End with a bang, not with a whimper.

In many cases it is advisable not to have a "technical" chapter called "Conclusion", but to end your dissertation with a concluding chapter, with its own substantial heading and content. The last section of that chapter may be an overall conclusion, but here again avoid repetition. You should summarize your points and probably suggest ways in which your conclusion can be thought of in a larger sense

---

[36] John W. Creswell, *Research Design*, p. 145.

The Appendices, if any

They contain other material that you consider relevant, referred to in the text of your work.

A Bibliography or Works Cited

Set out your comprehensive list of sources you have used in your research. Ensure that your bibliography is consistent. Differentiate Oral Sources, Unpublished Sources, Published Sources, and Web Sources.

Plagiarism

Plagiarism is a very serious offense although many people think of it as simply copying another person's work or borrowing someone else's work. The use of these terms, "copying" and "borrowing" disguises the seriousness of the offense of plagiarism.

The Meaning of Plagiarism

Plagiarism means:

1. Stealing and passing off the ideas or words of another as one's own
2. Using another's production without crediting the source
3. Committing literary theft
4. Presenting as new and original an idea or product deprived from an existing source (Merriam-Webster Online Dictionary)

Plagiarism is a very serious offence. It is an act of fraud which involves both stealing someone else's words and ideas

You must consider all of the following as plagiarism:

1. Handing in someone else's work as your own
2. Copying words or ideas from someone else without crediting or acknowledging the source
3. Failing to use quotation marks (" ") to show quoted words
4. Providing incorrect information about the source
5. Paraphrasing the sentence of ideas without acknowledging the source
6. Using ideas and words that make up a major part of your work with or without giving credit

However, many cases of plagiarism can be avoided by simply acknowledging the material that you have borrowed and providing your readers with the information necessary.

Images, Videos and Music

If you use an image, video or piece of music in your work without permission from the owners and acknowledging it properly amounts to plagiarism. Regardless of their popularity, the following are common examples of activities that are considered as plagiarism:

- Copying media, especially images, from other websites (which are not free to use) to paste them onto your own paper or website
- Making video using footage from other's videos or using copyrighted music as part of your soundtrack
- Performing another person's copyrighted music
- Composing a piece of music that borrows heavily from another person's or group's composition

These media can pose challenges to determine whether they have their copyrights violated. For example:

- A photograph or scan of a copyrighted image that is used, for example of a book cover to represent that book on one's website
- Recording audio or video in which copyrighted music or video is playing in the background
- Re-creating a visual work in the same medium, for example, shooting a photograph using the same composition and subject matter as someone else's photograph
- Re-creating a visual work in a different medium, for example, making a painting that closely resemble another's photography
- Re-mixing or altering copyrighted images, video or audio, even if done so in an original format

The legality of these situations and others would depend upon the intent and context in which they are produced. Two safest ways to take, in regards to these situations, are:

1. Acknowledge the source, and
2. Confirm the work's usage permissions and acknowledge them properly

Ten Most Common Types of Plagiarism

1. Submitting another person's work, word for word, as one's own
2. Presenting work that contains significant parts of text from a single source without acknowledging it
3. Changing key words and phrases but retaining the essential content of the source

4.   Paraphrasing from multiple sources made to fit together

5.   Borrowing generously from the writer's previous work without citation

6.   Combining perfectly cited sources with copied passage without citation

7.   Mixing copied material from multiple sources

8.   Including citations to non-existent sources or inaccurate information about sources

9.   Including proper citations to sources while the paper contains almost no original work.[37]

Plagiarism Policies and Procedures

Plagiarism is a problem that requires a clear statement regarding what is and what is not acceptable. The problem has been exacerbated by lack of understanding of incoming students about how to use other people's works in an academic exercise, and the easy access from the media, especially the Internet as discussed above. Although intellectual honesty and dishonesty are defined in different ways by different people,[38] the Plagiarism Policies and Procedures state just how seriously this institution takes using other person's work as one's own. "Doing right for right's sake is always right. It is always best."[39]

Procedures for Dealing with Plagiarism in Course Work

Let us look at how some universities deal with issues of plagiarism.

1.   When detecting plagiarism in a submitted work, the lecturer should warn the student verbally.

2.   When that happens again, the lecturer should warn the student in writing.

   a.   A copy of the letter should be sent to the head of department.

   b.   Another copy should be sent to the College Registrar who will file it in the student's personal file.

3.   The next time the lecturer detects plagiarism in the same student's coursework, she or he should refer the student to the Head of Department who should warn the student

   c.   The Head of Department will award a zero grade for the work.

   d.   A letter to the effect should be sent to the College Registrar for filling.

---

[37]   Plagiarism. http://www.plagiarism.org/plagiarism-101/what-is-plagiarism/ [11.11.2016]

[38]   N.J. Vyhmeister, *Quality Research Papers for Students of Religion and Theology*. Grand Rapids: Zondervan, 2008, p. 60.

[39]   N.J. Vyhmeister, *Quality Research Papers for Students of Religion and Theology*, p. 61.

Procedures for Dealing with Research Work

1. Supervisors and lecturers should take preventive and remedial action on any draft research work presented by students before the submission, particularly if the student has some legitimate educational problem of writing and referencing.

2. When a supervisor detects plagiarism in a submitted final draft before submission for examination, the supervisor should submit the matter to the Research Office's plagiarism committee so that the matter is dealt with internally.

3. When an internal or external examiner identifies potential plagiarism in research papers, the examiner should provide a thorough report indicating the nature and extent of potential plagiarism. The examiner should indicate the sources from which plagiarism has occurred. If possible, the institution should deal with the issue internally first.

4. For MA and PHD theses, the Head of Department (HOD) should refer allegations of plagiarism from examiners to the Dean of the Faculty. When the HOD or Dean is directly involved as supervisor/examiner, they should nominate a senior member of the Faculty to perform the task.

5. After considering the reports, the Dean must refer the matter to the Chair of the Plagiarism Committee. The Dean should inform the student who has all the rights with regard to the adjudication of the matter.

6. When there is no case of plagiarism, the Plagiarism Committee should refer the matter back to the HOD to make an academic recommendation on the result of the thesis in the light of other examiners' reports. The Dean of the Faculty will follow the ordinary procedures with regard to deciding the final result.

7. When the Plagiarism Committee finds that the student has committed plagiarism, the Committee should:

   a. Indicate the seriousness of the extent of the plagiarism, and
   b. Make recommendations with regard to the academic result.

8. In case of a Doctoral candidate being found guilty of plagiarism, the Plagiarism Committees' recommendations must be referred to the Vice Chancellor who will follow the ordinary procedures with regard to deciding the final academic result.[40]

Withdrawal of Degrees

It is not the wish of any University to withdraw research degrees conferred to its graduates. This is the last thing the university would do when it is discovered that your research paper is plagiarized greatly. This step will only be carried after thorough investigation and there is enough confirmation of pronounced plagiarism by the candidate.

---

[40] Rhodes University Higher Degrees Guide. Higherdegreesguide_08_09.pdf [5 July 2014].

When the Degree Awarding Committee of the Faculty feels that there is an obvious case of plagiarism, they will:

1. Refer the matter to the Senate Standing Committee on Plagiarism that is specifically constituted and empowered to hear the matter

2. Send the graduate the full particulars of the allegation with the allegedly plagiarized passages appropriately marked and documentary evidence of the original source material properly marked, too

3. Invite the graduate and the Head of the Department concerned

4. Give opportunity to the graduate to present evidence in support of the case

5. Have the right to ask questions

6. Consider its decision

7. Consider the penalty to be imposed

8. Recommend the revocation of the degree when they find the dissertation was adulterated by plagiarism

9. Provide the graduate with written reasons for its decision within five days of the hearing

10. Communicate to the Degree Awarding Committee when the Committee on Plagiarism recommends revocation of the degree.

The Degree Awarding Committee will direct the findings to the University Senate and Council for consideration and approval. They will compile a minute of the resolution, and make the reasons for the decision available to the graduate. The University Registrar will be responsible for communicating this information to the graduate.

When the deprivation of a degree is necessary, the Registrar will recall for the degree parchment from the student for destruction.[41]

As a student and a researcher you must know right away that plagiarism is not only a practice that is not acceptable, it is a sin and if you are found, the university will punish you. The university will either warn you, make you fail the course, suspend or expel you from the programme depending on the nature and seriousness of the offense. It does not matter whether you have not credited the source through carelessness or on purpose. "Ignorance has no defence." One way that helps to prevent unintentional plagiarism is careful note taking.[42] You must take note that any idea or phrase, whether spoken or written, regardless of where you pick it

---

[41] Rhodes University Higher Degrees Guide. Higherdegreesguide_08_09.pdf [5.7.2014].

[42] Randall VanderMey, Verne Meyer, John van Rys and Pat Sebranek, *The College Writer*, p. 447.

from, has its source acknowledged. That source could be another person, such as a fellow student, or your previous work, or an established writer, or a web reference for example. That is what it means to be a scholar.

Editing

Remember to present chapter by chapter to your supervisor for discussion and critical comments.[43] The supervisors are the ones who will declare that the student's work is complete; as a result, they will need to see the final version of the dissertation well before it is submitted for formal assessment.

When you edit, be unsympathetic with your work. Cut off anything that seems to have no direct relevance to your main idea or focus. It does not matter how good it sounds; as long as it does not make your point clear, chop it off. If it may be good for another assignment, put it on a "parking lot" to be used then. Replace passive statements with active ones. For example: you can replace "The ball was kicked by John" with "John kicked the ball."

Numbers

Always write a number in words if it appears at the beginning of a sentence. Numbers greater than twelve must be written in numerals. Write Bible references in numerals, for example, Gen 1:26, 2 Cor 2:11.

Tense

Although most research reports are written in the past tense, when referring to current truths use the present tense. Refer to information in a book always in the present tense.

Vocabulary and Sentence Structure

You must at all times keep your vocabulary and sentence structure simple and clear. Choose words that say precisely what you mean rather than choosing words that sound impressive or scholarly.

Quotations

There is a difference between quotations (or quotes) and references. The use of quotes should be restricted to cases of special importance. Most quotes are boring. Transform the information you are tempted to quote into your own words (suitable to your reader) and acknowledge the source appropriately.

---

[43] Often it may be advisable to present even smaller units, or drafts, or collection of source materials.

Save quotes from *secondary sources* to the very few cases where you feel that the text is so poignant that the reader must not get your words but the words of an authority beyond you. This is different with primary sources generated by your own research.

Quotes from *primary sources* may be useful and even needed to present the results of your research through "anecdotal evidence." Such subjective evidence must not be repetitive. Control the length of "anecdotal evidence quotes" by cutting out irrelevant phrases, but do not delete the personal and local flavour and repetitions.

If a quote is in the vernacular, normally put the English translation into the text and, if it adds value, the vernacular original into the footnote. For good reasons you may reverse the order, or, in cases of short quotes, put the English translation following the quote in brackets.

Make sure that a quote is *exactly* as the original, even including orthography.

If you want to leave out words, mark that with three dots[44] and omit any other punctuation marks. Do not start or finish a quote with three dots, since all quotes are cut from a larger text.

You may in certain cases insert your own words to clarify a quote by putting them into square brackets [ ].

If you want to point out a mistake or any other detail that needs attention, write [sic] in brackets. If there is a typing error with no further consequences, quietly correct it. Even if that is not in the text, you may change the first character of a quotation into a capital, and you may end the quotation with full stop.

Brief quotations are kept within the text (up to 2-3 lines). Set off longer quotes as "block quotes." Block quotations should be 10/15, indented 1 cm each side. The reference to the source of the quote is given in a footnote, of which the footnote number is placed at the end of the quotation, not at its beginning or where the quote is introduced.[45]

Completion and Submission of the Dissertation

You have completed your study after you have researched, written it and have submitted three copies to the Coordinator of Postgraduate Studies for onward transmission to approved external and internal examiners.

After receiving examiners reports, the Coordinator of Postgraduate Studies arranges for a viva voce where you defend the dissertation. The results are forwarded then to the Academic Postgraduate Committee that decides whether

---

[44] Put a space before and after the three dots, but not in between them. Klaus Fiedler, *Postgraduate Handbook*, p. 5.

your dissertation is accepted, pass or fail (and a grade is given in the case of an MA). The PhD is either pass or fail with no grade given.[46]

After the oral examination process is over, you are immediately informed of the results. If the work needs some adjustments, you are asked to do that guided by your supervisor and to the satisfaction of the Head of Department, before finally submitting to the Coordinator of Postgraduate Studies three hard-bound copies before the university can confer the degree to you.

Once that is done, what else, but to say, *Congratulations!*

---

[46] Another possible verdict is "Resubmit." This means that the thesis is not yet accepted, but that it may be resubmitted after necessary improvements have been made, usually within a specified and limited period.

Bibliography

Creswell, John W., *Research Design: Qualitative, Quantitative, and Mixed Methods Approaches*, Second Edition, Thousand Oaks: Sage, 2003

Fiedler, Klaus, *Postgraduate Handbook*, Department of Theology and Religious Studies 2011/2012, Mzuzu University, 2012.

Fraenkel, Jack R. and Norman E. Wallen, *How to Design and Evaluate Research in Education*, Boston: McGraw-Hill, 2000

Hacker, D., *A Writer's Reference with Exercises*, Boston: Bedford/St. Martins, 2008.

Mgomezulu, V.Y., and F.A. Kalua, *A Guide to Academic Writing for Beginners*, Mzuzu: Mzuni, Press, 2013

Mzuzu University, *Student Information Handbook,* Mzuzu: Mzuzu University, 2004.

Plagiarism, http://www.plagiarism.org/plagiarism-101/what-is-plagiarism/ [11.11.2014].

Rhodes University Higher Degrees Guide, Higherdegreesguide_08_09.pdf [5.7.2014]

Smith, Kevin Gary, *Academic Writing and Theological Research: A Guide for Students*, Johannesburg: South African Theological Seminary, 2008.

The Sunday School Board, *Bible Book Study Commentary – Matthew* (Part 2), Nashville: Convention Press, 1988.

VanderMey, Randall, Verne Meyer, John van Rys and Pat Sebranek, *The College Writer – A Guide to Thinking, Writing, and Research,* Second Edition. Boston: Houghton Mifflin, 2007.

Vyhmeister, N.J., *Quality Research Papers for Students of Religion and Theology*, Grand Rapids: Zondervan, 2008

Welch, Douglas E., Merle D. Strege and John H. Aukerman, *Guide to Theological Research and Writing*, Anderson: AU, 2010.

Printed in the United States
By Bookmasters